An American Looks At Wuerzburg, Germany

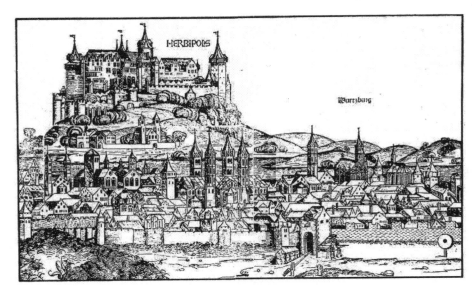

By
Catherine M. Jaime

Germany (country):

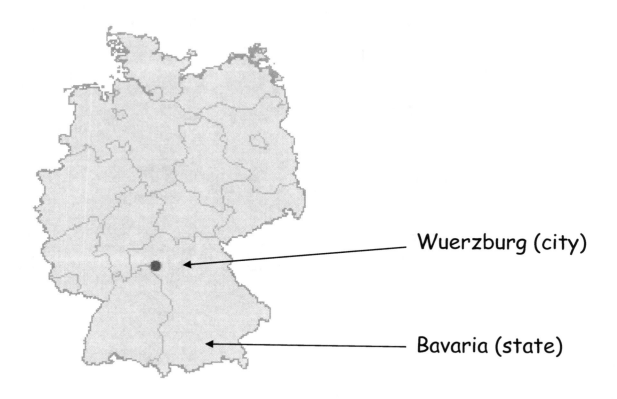

Wuerzburg (city)

Bavaria (state)

Creative Learning Connection
8006 Old Madison Pike, Ste 11-A
Madison, AL 35758
U.S.A.
www.CreativeLearningConnection.com

Table of Contents

Wuerzburg's Coat of Arms

Introduction to the Second Edition

Wuerzburg is a relatively small German city, on both sides of the Main River. It covers about 34 square miles, and has a population of about 134,000 people. It is located about 75 miles from Frankfurt, Germany and Nuremberg, Germany.

For many years after World War II, the Americans have had a presence in that city, with several small military bases. We were among the many Americans stationed there almost 20 years ago. We were stationed in Germany for 6 ½ years, first at the military base near Hanau, and then on the edge of Wuerzburg.

Before that time I had never really thought much about history! It was a subject I took in school. Something to memorize, take a test on, and then promptly forget. Wuerzburg changed all that. Suddenly history was exciting. It was interesting. And it was something I wanted to know more about.

And from that interest, came the beginnings of my first major writing project. I finished the first edition of this book a year or so before we left Germany. I self-published it, sold the first 100 copies, and then put it on a shelf, and almost forgot about it. Ten years later, in 2000, I started writing my second book, and then my third… Eventually I thought about bringing this book back into circulation.

My hope is that you enjoy this second edition, which contains only minor editorial changes, and many new illustrations, and that you will learn more about Wuerzburg and Germany in the process.

1990 Preface

This book comes to you as a work of love – the love an American has come to know over the past four years for a very special German city. It is not meant to be the last word on Wuerzburg. It is meant only to be an <u>introduction</u> to this amazing city.

To know and understand the history of Wuerzburg is to know and understand much of the history of Germany as a whole. This history is often difficult to grasp for Americans with a limited knowledge of German. This book originated from my frustrated attempts to find a book in English that covered the history of the Wuerzburg area in depth. As I added to my knowledge of Wuerzburg's history, and tried to relate what I did know to larger picture of German history, I dug deeper into whatever sources I could find: I pieced together information from books on sites of Wuerzburg; supplemented that with information found in several books on the history of Germany; and checked countless references in my encyclopedias and dictionaries. And after all that research, I came up with this book – sprinkled throughout with the marvelous tidbits I gleaned from numerous tours with Frau Helga Hoepffner, a wonderful German woman who gave me a great insight into Wuerzburg.

To Helga, I am indebted for an exciting introduction through her special English tours of the city, the castle, and the palace. She helped to instill in me a desire to learn as much as I could about this marvelous city. Other thanks go to my husband for his help with proofreading, and the rest of my family for putting up with me as my self-imposed deadline came closer. And a special thanks goes to a dear friend, LaDonna Wright, for encouragement and suggestions throughout the two years I first worked on this book.

A special thanks now to my daughter Maria who willingly retyped the entire book in 2008 when we thought seriously of re-publishing it!

Last, but not least, a special thanks to my Lord, who has given us a world with such beauty that we may enjoy.

I hope you enjoy this book and this city as I have.

Note: Because this started as an informal work, I have chosen an informal method for my footnotes. My references are listed in the back and are numbered. Footnotes are labeled with the number of their source, and the page number from that source.

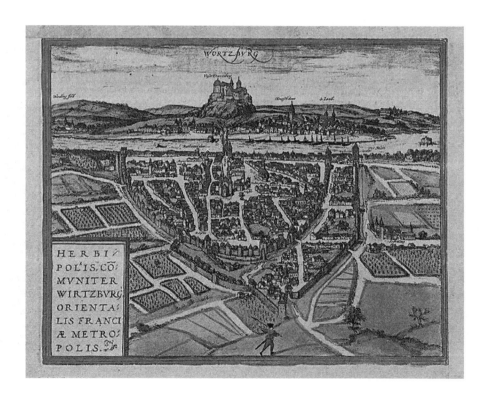

Chapter One
A Brief Guide to Wuerzburg's History

Introduction

In order to put the events of **Wuerzburg** into proper historical perspective, I have included throughout these pages brief summaries of relative portions of **Germany's** history. To make it easier for the reader to follow these different portions throughout this chapter, I have used the following markings:

//
DENOTES SPECIAL DATES IN GERMANY'S HISTORY
//

DENOTES APPROXIMATE DATES OF ART/ARCHICTECTURE

(Denotes part of local folklore)

[Denotes historic tidbits]

Denotes explanations of German history

Hopefully, these symbols will enable the reader to gain a better understanding of both Wuerzburg's history and Germany's history!

1000 BC Wuerzburg was a Celtic fishing settlement along the Main River 3,000 years ago. Even then there was a small "fortified" area on the hilltop where the Marienberg Fortress now stands.

1st Century BC Roman soldiers were in and out of Southern Germany in the century before Christ. Roman invasions of these areas were especially heavy under Julius Caesar and Emperor Augustus. During that time, a Roman camp was located on the hilltop in "Old Wuerzburg".[1]

Julius Caesar

Emperor Augustus

///
~500 A.D. - 1000 A.D. THE DARK AGES
(Also considered the first half of the MIDDLE AGES)
///

The Dark Ages began as the invading Barbarian tribes throughout Europe brought an end to the Roman Empire.

500 AD During the Germanic migration at the beginning of the Middle Ages, many tribes moved through this area. Members of the Franconian tribe finally settled here, driving out the Celtics. The Franconians built a place of pagan worship on the Marienberg (hilltop), and soon added a wall around it for protection.

---

[1] 7 – pg 148

Irish monks began to Christianize Germany in 600 A.D.

686 Bishop Kilian and his companions, Kolonat and Totnan, came from Ireland as missionaries to Christianize the Franconian area. By this time the Frankish Duke in Wuerzburg, Duke Hetan I, had moved his estate to the other side of the river, in about the area of the Kilianplatz. *Kilian baptized the Duke, but refused to baptize his wife, Gallana.[2] He claimed she was "living in sin", since she had married the brother of her late husband.*

689 *While the Duke was away at battle, his wife and two of her servants killed the three missionaries and hid their bodies under a horse stable.*

705 Duke Hetan II (Gallana's son) became the new ruler of Franconia. He built the Marienkirche as a chapel and defensive post on the hilltop of "Old Wuerzburg". Located now in the midst of the Marienberg Fortress, it was the only building on the hill at the time, predating the rest of the fortress by more than 500 years. [The Marienkirche is now the oldest church in Germany east of the Rhine River.]

739 *50 years after the slaying of Kilian and his companions, their bodies were finally discovered. <u>Two different legends</u> have come about to explain the discovery...*

> *1. People had noticed that the horses in a certain stable, near the Kilianplatz, always avoided one spot of the ground, but no knew why. One day a blind boy "saw" a stream of blood coming out of the ground.[3]*

---

[2] 11 - pg 81
[3] 1

or

2. A man digging on the Marienberg suddenly saw blood gushing from the ground.[4]

…The area was then dug up and the bodies of the three missionaries were found.

742 St. Boniface, an English archbishop just north of Wuerzburg at Fulda, established Wuerzburg as a bishopric.[5] He installed the first bishop of Wuerzburg, Bishop Burkard.

St. Boniface

748 Bishop Burkard founded the first monastery in the area – at the base of the hill, below the Marienkirche.

****Pepin the Short was the first Frankish ruler to call himself king.[6]
His son Charles the Great (Charlemagne) went on to rule most of
central and western Europe.****

///
768-814 CHARLEMAGNE RULED THE GERMAN EMPIRE
///

---

[4] 8 - pg 6
[5] A bishopric is a "territory under the jurisdiction of a bishop"
[6] 8 - pg 5

787 Charlemagne visited Wuerzburg.

788 The Marienkirche had become too small for Wuerzburg's growing population, so the first cathedral was built in Wuerzburg, located downtown on the site of the present Neumuenster Church. Charlemagne was present for the dedication.

791 Charlemagne visited Wuerzburg a third time.

///
800 CHARLEMAGNE CROWNED EMPEROR
///

Charlemagne allowed himself to be crowned Emperor by Pope Leo III. Together they created a new church-state, the German Empire, which was held together until his death.

Charlemagne

///
800-1806 THE FIRST REICH (EMPIRE)
///

The Treaty of Verdun was signed in 843, shortly after Charlemagne's death. It settled the squabble between his grandsons over the empire. The areas of France and Germany were divided.

11

855 The first cathedral in Wuerzburg had been destroyed previously by lightening. In 855 it was replaced by a new cathedral, this one in the area of the present Dom (the church that would be built there in the next two centuries).

Otto I revived Charlemagne's imperial title when he was crowned "King of the Franks and the Lombards" in Rome in 962.[7] Even as Emperor he had limited powers in a land where Counts and later Prince Bishops (see the year 1168) held the real power at the local level.

Otto I

1000 The first wall was built around the city of Wuerzburg.

1034 The building of the Dom was begun by Bishop Bruno. (The second cathedral had also been destroyed by fire.) It is THE main church of Wuerzburg, "the bishop's church".

1035 St. Burkard Church developed from the monastery Bishop Burkard had begun several centuries earlier. It was consecrated by Bishop Bruno and is one of Wuerzburg's oldest churches.

---

[7] 5 - pg 15

1050-1250 ROMANESQUE STYLE

Example of Romanesque Style Architecture

**During the Middle Ages, building was mainly done by the leaders – both ecclesiastical (church) and secular (kings, princes, etc.).

As the Dark Ages ended, the first distinctive style of building in Europe, the Romanesque style, developed. Romanesque buildings tended to have a very heavy and very gloomy appearance, often with towers at both ends.**

//
1096-1270 CRUSADES TO THE HOLY LAND
//

The Crusades were a set of loosely organized attempts by Christian soldiers from Western Europe to take Jerusalem back from the Turks. For the next two centuries, there were seven such expeditions to the Holy Land. Even though the crusades were never successful in liberating Jerusalem, they did succeed in establishing the orders of the Knights (i.e. the Teutonic Knights and the Knights Hospitaller) as political entities in the Medieval World.

Coat of Arms – Teutonic Knights

1133 Wuerzburg had developed on both sides of the Main River and the first stone bridge was built in this part of Germany, the "Alte Mainbrucke".

//
1152-1190 BARBAROSSA RULED THE GERMAN EMPIRE
//

During Barbarossa's rule, the term "Holy Roman Empire" was first applied to the German Empire.[8] (Not to be confused with the <u>Roman</u> Empire that existed before the Middle Ages, the <u>Holy Roman</u> Empire had its center in the <u>Roman Catholic Church,</u> not in the geographic location of <u>Rome</u>!)

---

[8] 5 - pg 16

1156   Emperor Barbarossa (Frederick Red Beard), the second Emperor of the German Empire, came to Wuerzburg for his marriage to Beatrice of Burgundy. [He was 31, she was 12.]

Emperor Barbarossa

1168   Emperor Barbarossa gave the Bishop of Wuerzburg the additional title of Duke of Franconia, making him Wuerzburg's first Prince Bishop.[9] Thus began the 650 year rule (1168-1802) of the Prince Bishops of Wuerzburg.

1188   The Dom was finally consecrated, more than 100 years after building had begun. Like most churches built at this time, the Dom was built in the shape of a cross.

1190   One of Wuerzburg's Prince Bishops, Prince Bishop Spitzenberg, died on a Crusade.

///
1198-1214 Civil War in the German Empire over next Emperor
///

---

9 As Prince Bishops, they were leaders of both the local church and government.

1200 As the importance of towns in the Empire increased, so did Wuerzburg's importance. With its growing significance, came expansion. A new wall was built around Wuerzburg at this time, enclosing a larger area. This wall had the zig zag shape that is still evident downtown today, in the "Ring Park".

1201 Wuerzburg's Prince Bishop Konrad von Querfurt sided with Otto of Brunswick in the Civil War. He began the foundation of the Marienberg Fortress as protection against the troops of French King Phillip; and built the keep at the fortress at this time. At this time the area of the fortress became known as "Marienberg" instead of "Old Wuerzburg".

King Phillip II (on the right) meeting with the Pope

1221 The Franciscan Monastery in Wuerzburg was the first Franciscan Monastery outside of Italy.

Walther von der Vogelweide

1230 The famous German minstrel, Walther von der Vogelweide, was buried at the Lusam Garden. Walther von der Vogelweide had been known throughout the Empire for his love songs.

1250-1500 Gothic Style

Example of Gothic Architecture

Buildings during the Gothic period were taller and more graceful than they had been during Romanesque. Stained glass windows became extremely popular during this time.

//
1250-1273 The "Great Interregnum"
//

An interregnum is the interval of time between the end of a sovereign's reign and the accession of a successor. During this time in the 13th century, the German Empire was in a state of turmoil after the loss of its emperor, Frederick II. Citizens of Wuerzburg and other major Franconian towns struggled to break the bonds with their local leaders, in Wuerzburg's case - the Prince Bishops, and show their loyalty directly to the emperor.

Frederick II

1253 Prince Bishop Lodeburg moved from town to the Marienberg Fortress to escape the wrath of the townspeople who were loyal to the Emperor. This castle continued to be the official residence for Wuerzburg's Prince Bishops until 1720.

Gunpowder was developed at the beginning of the 14th century. It hastened the end of the Middle Ages, soon making the fortified castles of that time obsolete.

1316 The Grafeneckart, built in 1200, became the Rathaus (the Town Hall).

Rathaus, shown at the end of the street.

1319 The hospital known as the Buergerspital zum Heiligen Geist was founded. For over 600 years, it provided care to the elderly of Wuerzburg.

A form of Bubonic Plague, the "Black Death", killed a quarter of the population in Europe between 1334 and 1351. It was most likely brought to Europe by the Crusaders.

1349 In Wuerzburg the Plague started in the Jewish ghetto - where the Marktplatz is now located. The townspeople blamed the Jews for the plague, and burned the entire area to the ground. It was later determined that this was the lowest point in town, and all the sewage was draining there; the real reason the plague started there.

1377 The townspeople regretted the destruction of the Jewish area, and donated money to build a church there. Thus the Marienkapelle was begun as a "citizen's church". It was built where the Jewish synagogue had been located. Erected in the 14th and 15th centuries (1377-1480), it is one of the few Gothic style buildings left in Wuerzburg.

1397 *King Wenceslas, the Polish King to whom Wuerzburg citizens paid taxes, visited Wuerzburg. A reception was given for him in the hall on the second floor of the Rathaus. He promptly decided Wuerzburg was one of his favorite cities, and promised her citizens they would not have to pay him taxes anymore. From Wuerzburg, he went to Frankfurt, where he was declared insane and forced to abdicate. Wuerzburg was once again subject to taxation, but they named the Wenceslas Hall of the Rathaus after the "Good King" anyway.*[10]

---

[10] 1 & 11 - pg 66

1402 The "Old University" was founded, the fourth university to start in Germany.[11] It was closed by student riots in 1413.

1450-1600 German Renaissance

Although the Renaissance had begun in Italy about 1300, it took another 150 years to reach Germany. Even more than at other times, the Italian influence was seen in German buildings during the time of the Renaissance.[12]

//
1447 Gutenberg printed the first book from movable metal types, in Mainz, Germany, about 100 miles from Wuerzburg.
//

In 1453 the first major work was printed on Gutenberg's press, the Bible.

"Old Saints' Bridge"

---

[11] 14 - pg 33
[12] 5 - pg 20

1473 The Alte Mainbrucke (often referred to by Americans as the "Old Saints Bridge") was rebuilt in its present form.

1478 German sculptor Tilman Riemenschneider came to Wuerzburg for the first time as an 18-year-old boy. His uncle was the financial advisor to Wuerzburg's Prince Bishop. To fulfill the requirement of his guild, he left Wuerzburg to travel. Among other places, he visited the wood-carving workshops of Swabia and the upper Rhine.[13]

1481 Wuerzburg had her first book printer. Germans were fast becoming the printers of Europe.

1483 Riemenschneider returned to Wuerzburg, having reached the level of "journeyman".

1485 Riemenschneider married the widow of a goldsmith. He gained her late husband's title of "master" with the marriage. With the title, came the right to open up a workshop.[14]

1493 Riemenschneider made his first works for the city of Wuerzburg, life-size statues of Adam and Eve. Although his favorite medium was lime wood, these statues like many others, were made of sandstone. He also made many wood sculptures.[15]

---

[13] 9 - pg 4
[14] 9 - pg 4
[15] 6 - pg 98

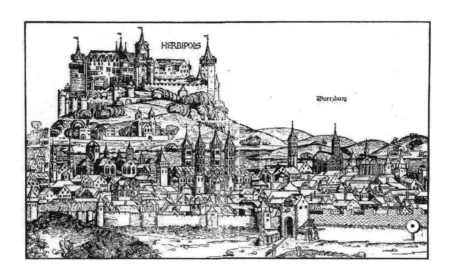

Wuerzburg in 1493

//
The End of the Middle Ages
//

Several things helped bring the time we call "the Middle Ages" to an end. These included the discovery of the New World, the Crusades and the trade with the Near East they brought; the growing strength of towns and cities, and the diminishing power of the Catholic Church.

1505 Riemenschneider began his civil career with a position on Wuerzburg's town council.[16]

//
1517 The Reformation Began
//

---

[16] 9 - pg 4

During the Middle Ages the Catholic Church had been the number one power throughout most of Europe. Reformers for several centuries before Martin Luther had challenged the authority of the Church. When Luther also tried to reform his German church with his "Ninety-Five Theses" nailed to its door in 1517, the Reformation officially began.

Martin Luther

1518 Martin Luther visited Prince Bishop Lorenz von Bibra at the Marienberg.[17] (Luther was most likely on his way to or from Augsburg.)

1520 Riemenschneider was elected mayor of Wuerzburg by her citizens.

///
1524-1526 Peasants War
///

Peasants throughout the German Empire had become increasingly more upset for several decades over the demands of their lords. Luther's preaching served to spark the flames of their growing dissatisfaction. They rose up in rebellion against their rulers, hoping to find an ally in Luther. He rejected their cries for help, effectively crushing any chance the peasants had of winning.

---

[17] 13 - pg 34

1525 During the Peasants' War, the peasants in the Wuerzburg area rose up under the leadership of Florian Geyer. They tried unsuccessfully to chase Prince Bishop Konrad von Thuengen out of Wuerzburg. Riemenschneider sided with the peasants and was imprisoned for a while in the bottom of a tower at the castle.

Florian Geyer

1531 Tilman Riemenschneider died in Wuerzburg, leaving behind countless world-famous statues, tombs, and altars. He is considered today to have been one of the leaders of Gothic art in Germany.

1576 The Juliusspital (a hospital/old people's home) was founded by Prince Bishop Julius Echter von Mespelbrunn.

1582 The Old University was reopened by Prince Bishop Julius Echter von Mespelbrunn.

1600 Much of the castle had been destroyed by fires in 1572 and 1600. Prince Bishop von Mespelbrunn rebuilt his home at the Marienberg in the fancier Renaissance style, giving it its current shape.

1600-1800 Baroque Style

The Baroque style of architecture flourished in Bavaria. The churches built during this time usually contained elaborate facades, altarpieces, and frescoes. Staircases were an important part of the palaces built then.[18]

Example of Baroque Architecture

///
1618-1648 Thirty Years' War
///

The Thirty Years' War was the last major religious war in Europe. It began as a war between the Catholics and Protestants across the German Empire, stemming from conflicts going back to Luther's Reformation. Denmark, Sweden, and France eventually entered on the side of the Protestants. During the Thirty Years' War, every major city in the German Empire, except Vienna and Hamburg, was occupied at some time by hostile armies. By the end of the conflict, more than a third of the population in Germany had been killed.[19]

1631 The Marienberg Fortress was conquered for the first time. Soldiers were sneaking out of the fortress to get more help, and were shot on the drawbridge. Their bodies were too heavy, and the soldiers inside could not lift the drawbridge back up.[20] Marienberg remained in the hands of the Swedish Army until the Emperor's Army regained it in 1635.

---

[18] 5 - pg 20, 21
[19] 8 - pg 5
[20] 13 - pg 16

The Thirty Years' War ended with a peace treaty that was in effect for the next 150 years. This treaty, the Peace of Westphalia, settled the issue of Catholics and Protestants getting along, by marking every city entirely Catholic or entirely Protestant. Wuerzburg, of course, became Catholic. Under this treaty, Protestants, Jews, and Gypsies could not live inside Wuerzburg's wall. They could come in during the day to do business, but had to be outside by nightfall. Heidingsfeld, about two miles southeast of Wuerzburg, was an enclave for these restricted groups, and contains an old Jewish cemetery, and a Christian cemetery, with Gypsy tombs surrounding the outside.

1642 The first Prince Bishop of Wuerzburg from the Schoenborn family was elected. (The Schoenborn family went on to become famous for their Baroque building ventures, in particular the Wuerzburg Residenz.) Even as the Thirty Years' War was winding down, Prince Bishop Johann Philipp Schoenborn expanded the fortifications at the Marienberg.

1711 Balthasar Neumann, an inspiring architect, came to Wuerzburg as an 18-year-old apprentice to a bell-founder.

1711 An addition was made to Neumuenster Church, because the Prince Bishop wanted a "grander style" church. The first section was rather plain, in Romanesque style, compared to the Baroque style of the addition.

1712 An arsenal is added to the castle (Marienberg).

1714 At the beginning of his reign, Prince Bishop Johann Philip Franz von Schoenborn of Wuerzburg decided he needed a more splendid palace to live in, instead of the castle on the hill. He was confident that his court architect, Balthasar Neumann, although still an unknown in the world of architecture, could handle his great building project. So, he ordered him to prepare plans for his new Residenz immediately![21]

Towards the end of the Baroque period, a form of art called Rococo became popular. Rococo art was generally more delicate than the Baroque art it replaced.

Example of Rococo Architecture

1720 The Prince Bishop himself laid the cornerstone for the Residenz, even though the plans were still incomplete. (The plans were very European in flavor, with experts from Germany, France, Italy, Australia, and Holland contributing to Neumann's overall plans.)[22] The Prince Bishop then moved down to the Hof Rosenbach, near the Residenz, so he could watch the progress.

1724 Prince Bishop von Schoenborn died with only one-fifth of his palace completed. He was replaced by von Hutten, who was not interested in continuing work on the Residenz.[23] (However, von Hutten did have the first six statues added to the Alte Mainbrucke or "Old Saints' Bridge".)

---

[21] 10 - pg 6
[22] 10 - pg 15
[23] 11 - pg 23

Old Saint's Bridge

1729 Prince Bishop von Hutten died and was replaced by another member of the Schoenborn family. Work was resumed on the Residenz quickly. Emphasis was on the completion of the building itself, but some interior work was done as well. Prince Bishop Friedrich Karl von Schoenborn also started work on the second half of the Alte Mainbrucke statues.

1737 The famous double staircase at the Residenz was finished.

1743 Neumann's Court Chapel at the Residenz was finally consecrated and the flat-vaulted ceiling over the staircase was completed.

1744 "24 years after the laying of the foundation stone" of the Residenz, "the skeleton of the building was (finally) completed. A feast of thanksgiving was held and 16 Masses were held."[24]

---

[24] 10 - pg 13

1745 Maria Theresa, the Austrian empress, stayed overnight at the Residenz on her way through Wuerzburg. Her husband was about to be crowned Emperor in Frankfurt. Much of the Residenz, including the great staircase, the Imperial Hall, and most of the Parade Room were unfinished. Maria Theresa's first reaction to the Residenz was not good. But when she saw the Mirror Hall, all that was incomplete was forgotten. The magnificence of this hall, with its mirrors, gold-plating, and reverse-glass painting,[25] more than made up for what was yet undone. It was after seeing this room that the Empress reportedly said, "This is the palace of palaces!"[26]

Austrian Empress Maria Theresa   *Holy Roman Emperor Frances I*

1746 The left wing of the Residenz was finished, and the Prince Bishop finally moved in. Shortly after moving in, Prince Bishop Friedrich Karl von Schoenborn died, leaving the completion of the Residenz once again up in the air. The new Prince Bishop was not interested in the building project, and had Neumann dismissed from his position as court architect.

1748 During his break from the Residenz, Neumann began building the Kaeppele, the "Little Chapel". It was built across the Main River on the site of a former pilgrim's chapel, and continues to draw many pilgrims.

---

25 Reverse-glass painting (painting on the underside of viewed glass) was popular in 18th century Europe.

[26] 2 - pg 68

Kaeppele

1749 The interruption to the Residenz work was brief this time. The latest Prince Bishop died and was replaced by Prince Bishop von Greiffenklau. This latest in the long line of Prince Bishops to work on the Residenz was not a member of the Schoenborn family, but he shared their building ideas. Neumann was reinstated as court architect, and was able to get on with plans for Court Garden and the interior decoration of the Residenz.

1750 Giovanni Battista Tiepolo, a "leading rococo painter"[27], arrived from Italy with his two sons. During the next three years Tiepolo painted the largest ceiling painting in the world at the Residenz.[28]

1753 Neumann died, before the Residenz had been completely decorated. But he did see his dream of a magnificent palace in Wuerzburg come true. He is buried in the Marienkapelle.

1765 The Four Pipes Fountain, the "Vierroehrenbrunnen", was built in front of the Rathaus. It is an original, not having been destroyed in the air raid. (This air raid of World War II is explained briefly at the end of this chapter and in more detail at the end of the second chapter.) When the Emperor visited, and when Prince Bishops were elected, it was filled with wine.

---

[27] 3-QR - pg 369
[28] 8 - pg 35

1767   The Main River Crane was begun by Neumann's son, Franz Ignatz, at the center of Wuerzburg's harbor.

1770   The gardens at the Residenz were finally begun. Since the gardens were very limited in size by the city fortifications behind the Residenz, the usual French design was not possible. The smaller section behind the Residenz was to be done in Italian style, and the larger sections to the side of the Residenz were to be done in the Austrian style of the day. But by the time the gardens were done, English landscaping had changed the world of landscape design, and the gardens followed the English style more than any other. The statues in the gardens were done by Johann Georg Oegg and his son, also well-known at that time.

1771 The Legation Wing was built on the south side of the Residenz Square - a copy of the Hof Rosenbach that stood opposite it.

1796   French revolutionary soldiers were defeated outside Wuerzburg on their first attempt to take the city.

///
1799 - 1813 Napoleonic Wars
///

When Napoleon I took power in France, he proceeded to dominate most of Europe for the next twenty years. He quickly put an end to the Church's power and ended the peace treaty from the Thirty Years' War that had required each city to maintain a single "allowable" religion.

1800 Napoleon's French Revolutionary Army successfully entered Wuerzburg for the first time. The Marienberg Fortress once again fell into enemy hands, where it remained for several years.

1802 In light of Napoleon's growing power and anti-church attitude, Prince Bishop Fehrenbach abdicated, ending the 650 year rule of Prince Bishops in Wuerzburg.

1803 Wuerzburg lost her rights as a free city and became part of the state of Bavaria.

The Bavarian State Coat of Arms

1806 Napoleon stayed at the Residenz on a visit to Wuerzburg. During this same year he officially dissolved the Holy Roman Empire.

1815 Crown Prince Ludwig I resided in Wuerzburg until he was made King of Bavaria by Napoleon in 1825. His son, Luitpold, was born at the Residenz during this time (1821).

1817 The Koenig & Bauer factory was founded in Wuerzburg. They still make high-quality, high-speed printing machines, one of which printed dollars in the U.S. for many years.

1821 Ludwig had Oegg's wrought iron screen gate in front of the Residenz removed and dismantled, leaving an unsightly gap.

1837 A Jewish synagogue was built across from the Old University.

A German Confederation of thirty-five states and towns was set in place to replace the government lost with the dissolving of the Holy Roman Empire. Frankfurt am Main was set up as the center of this government.[29]

1853 Wuerzburg was connected to the new railway system in Germany.[30]

1866 During the Austro-Prussian War, the Marienberg Fortress proved to be no match for the modern weapons of the Prussian artillery. By the next year, its function as a fortress was finished.

//
1870-1871 Bismarck United Germany
//

Otto von Bismarck, as the Minister-President of Prussia, had managed to bring the northern states of Germany together as one unit in the early 1860s. He was finally successful at bringing the southern states into unity with them in 1870.[31]

---

[29] 5 - pg 17
[30] 8 - pg 7

//
1871-1918 The Second Reich
//

1871 The city wall was torn down and the moat was filled in so Wuerzburg could expand. A tower from the wall remains; it is now part of the University. A park, the Ring Park, was constructed in place of the wall and moat.

1894 Wuerzburg's citizens installed the Franconian Fountain in front of the Residenz - where the gate had been. The fountain has statues of three of Franconia's most famous sons - Riemenschneider (the sculptor), Gruenewald (the painter), and Vogelweide (the minstrel). Above them stands the patroness of Franconia.

1895 X-rays were discovered at the Juliusspital by Wilhelm Conrad Roentgen.

//
1914-1918 World War I
//

After World War I, Marienberg was used as temporary housing for displaced civilians in Wuerzburg.

//
1933-1945 The Third Reich
//

[31] 5 - pg 17

1938 The Synagogue across from the Old University was destroyed on November 9, "Crystal Night", the "Night of Broken Glass", as part of a horrendous destruction of Jewish synagogues all over Germany; part of the rise of Anti-Semitic persecution of the Jews in Germany.

1939 Restoration of the castle had been completed. (Only to be undone by the air raid during World War II.)

//
1939-1945 World War II
//

1945 March 16, 1945 - Six weeks before the end of the war, Wuerzburg was bombed. Eighty-five percent of Wuerzburg was destroyed in the air raid. There were 700 attacks, in 20 minutes, by 236 bombers from the RAF Bomber Command. They dropped 600 exploding bombs and 400 air mines. The surface of the river even burned. More than 5000 people were killed, most of whom are buried in a mass grave near the Berliner Ring.

April 5, 1945 - Two weeks after the air raid the Americans entered Wuerzburg. The city was still in flames, and the destruction was so great they called Wuerzburg "the tomb at the Main". Serious consideration was given to leveling the city and rebuilding it downriver at Veitshoechheim. Fortunately, that plan was dropped, and massive repairs were done on Wuerzburg's buildings instead. Much of the city has been rebuilt to its original glory.

1947 Marienberg's Arsenal became home to the Mainfraenkische Museum.

1983 At Easter time Wuerzburg's Jewish community donated a menorah to the Catholic and Protestant citizens of Wuerzburg. It was to be considered a sign of friendship, but not of forgiveness. It stands inside the front door of the Dom.

The timeline on the back page sums up the main dates from this chapter.

Chapter Two
An Alphabetical Guide
to Wuerzburg's Sites and People

Introduction

This chapter gives more details on the major sites in Wuerzburg, and includes more of the colorful stories about this fascinating city.

One interesting story involves the meaning of Wuerzburg's name. The hill where the Marienberg Fortress stands has had herbs growing on it for many centuries. So the names "Wuerzburg" ("Wuerz" means "spicy herbs") and Herbipolis are similar names for this city. Actually, one could say "Wuerzburg" means "castle of herbs" and "Herbipolis" means "city of herbs". That explains why, on old pictures of Wuerzburg, one so often finds the name "Herbipolis":

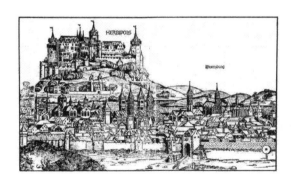

Another interesting fact from former days is the way different trades would be located together. For example, Schmalzmarkt means "lard market" and Schustergasse means "shoe maker street". SemmelStrasse, the "baker's street", was outside of the city fortifications, because of the ovens. They were too dangerous to be near the wooden buildings.

I hope you enjoy this brief look at the following attractions and personalities of Wuerzburg:

* 1. Alte Mainbrucke ("Old Saints Bridge")
* 2. Alter Kranen (Main River Crane)
* 3. Buergerspital
* 4. Dom
* 5. Falkenhaus
* 6. Franciscan Monastery
* 7. Juliusspital
* 8. Kaeppele
* 9. Lusamgarten
*11. Marienberg Fortress
*10. Mainfraenkische Museum
*12. Marienkapelle
*13. Neumann, Balthasar
*14. Neumuenster Church
*15. Old University
*16. Rathaus
*17. Residenz
*18. Riemenschneider, Tilman
*19. St. Burkard Church
*20. World War II

1. Alte Mainbrucke ("Old Saints' Bridge)

The Old Main Bridge, or "Old Saints' Bridge", was originally built in 1133. It was built in its present form from 1473 to 1543.

During the Middle Ages, the bridge was the only connection between the castle and the town. Since Wuerzburg was surrounded by a wall, the bridge was the only way to enter or leave. There was a toll gate at the end, where travelers paid a fee to cross.

The 12 saints' statutes were added to the sides of the bridge between 1724 and 1746. Prince Bishop von Hutten commissioned the work for the saints on the south side of the bridge first. Then Prince Bishop Friedrich Karl von Schoenborn had the saints on the north side of the bridge designed.[32] Three of the south side statues should be familiar to anyone knowledgeable of Wuerzburg's history: the three martyred saints -- Kilian, Kolonat, and Totnan. Another statue on that side is Franconia, the patroness saint of this area. The last two there were both bishops - Burkard (the first bishop in Wuerzburg) and Bruno (one of the most famous bishops). The statues on the north side are not as familiar. Two of them commemorate the Franconian tribal leaders - Pepin the Short and his son Charlemagne. (So far so good.) And one of the middle statues on that side is actually of two people - Joseph and Jesus (as a young boy).

---

[32] 11 - pg 84

The remaining three are of saints - their Latin names are "Carlos Borromaus", "Johann von Nepomuk", and "Friedericus".

Again, there are two slightly different stories surrounding these statues:

1) That the statues on the bridge survived the air raid during World War II with minimal damage; only the gold on the swords and halos melted and had to be replaced. After the bombing, when the Americans were trying to enter the city, the angry citizens of Wuerzburg bombed their side of the bridge. They did not succeed in knocking even one of the statues into the River![33]

2) Another source says that several of the statues were damaged during the war, when retreating German troops blew up the central piers of the bridge. Actually, those damaged statues were reproductions from the beginning of the century.

…Either way, the Alte Mainbrucke is once again complete with its Baroque statues of 12 saints.

---
[33] 1

2. Alter Kranen (Main River Crane)

The crane was built by Balthasar Neumann's son between 1767 and 1773. Its location was the center of the harbor at the time.

The crane was commissioned by Prince Bishop Seinsheim to increase the city's loading efficiency.[34] It loaded and unloaded boats at the same time, since it was two-sided. It was turned by manpowered treadmills that still work.

The crane has a Latin inscription which means, "I receive, transport, and dispatch anything you like."

---

[34] 11 - pg79

3. Buergerspital

In 1319 the Buergerspital zum Heiligen Geist, often called just the "Holy Ghost Hospice", was founded as an old people's home. Several vineyards were donated to it, so it could support itself. These are among the many Franconian vineyards that use the famous "Bocksbeutel"- the unusually shaped wine bottles so popular in this area. The Buergerspital now has the third largest winery in Germany.

The glockenspiel (clock) at the Buergerspital goes off at 11 a.m., 1 p.m., 3 p.m., and 5 p.m. It shows the three missionaries, Calvary pilgrims, the Franconian wine queen, and a dove, which is the symbol of the home.

4. Dom

The Dom is formally called "The Cathedral of St. Kilian". It is the "bishop's church", now the main church of Wuerzburg. It was built in the 11th and 12th centuries on the site of a 9th century cathedral and is one of the largest Romanesque churches in Germany. There were no pews in it when it was built, and more than 5,000 people could fit, standing to worship there. When pilgrims came to the area, they could also sleep in the church.

At the beginning of the 18th century the little church at the back of the Dom - the Schoenborn Tomb Chapel - was added by the same family that built the Residenz. The chapel is decorated with baby angels, representing birth, and skeletons, representing death.

The bronze front door of the Dom is a modern addition that shows God creating the world.

After being almost completely rebuilt after World War II, the exterior of the Dom has maintained its Romanesque style, but the interior has undergone many changes. The 22 wooden altars that had been in the Dom all burned. The bells in the steeple melted down the steps of the tower and ruined the treasures that had been stored there. The HUGE crucifix by Riemenschneider also burned. It had been at least twice as big as the modern cross hanging above the main altar now.

One of the church treasures that survived the air raid is in the Baptism Chapel, on the right side of the front door. The bronze baptismal there was made in 1279. The inside of the baptismal is done as **one** piece; the largest such baptismal in Germany.

The reliefs around the Baptismal show:
1. The angel telling Mary about the Virgin Birth
2. Birth of Christ: Mary (lying down), baby, Joseph
3. Baptism of Christ
4. Crucifixion (with devil and mourning angel)
5. Christ coming out of tomb
6. Ascension of Christ - see His feet and footprints
7. Pentecost-Mary and disciples and flames
8. Last Judgment: Christ on throne, angels with script, Mary, John

The skulls of Wuerzburg's three martyred patron saints (Kilian, Kolonat, and Totan) are kept in the Dom's main altar. Each year from the Sunday before July 8 (Kiliani Day - believed to be the date of their deaths) to the Sunday after, the skulls are brought out and put on display.

5. Falkenhaus

Once a gasthaus (guest house), the Falkenhaus is now the property of the city and contains a City Library and a Tourist Office. It is a rather plain structure, but with beautiful rococo decorations on its front. The story goes: *stucco workers from the Residenz lived at the Falkenhaus in the 18th century. They owed the owner too much money after running up large tabs for their food and drink and were unable to pay their bills, so they decorated the front of the building in 1751 to pay off their bills.*

6. Franciscan Monastery

The Franciscan Order is a "poverty" order. There are no impressive towers, steeples, or bells since the members prefer to donate their money to the needy. The monks have been nicknamed "barefoot monks".

The Monastery here was started in the early part of the 13th century while St. Francis was still alive. It moved to its present location later in the 13th century. The Monastery Gardens are a link between styles: the plain arches on the side are late Romanesque; and the arches on the ends are early Gothic - built 30 years later.

Americans bombed Wuerzburg briefly in February 1945, trying to hit the SS HQ located in the River Building. They hit the monastery instead and it suffered minor damage. During the air raid in March it was almost totally destroyed. The garden and one hallway are all that's left of the original structure. The headpiece of the bomb that hit the Monastery is on display there.

There are vestments kept in the monastery that are several hundred years old. They were moved to another monastery before the air raid, and were saved from being destroyed.

The monastery was rebuilt after the war and had to be rebuilt yet again after a major fire in 1986.

St Francis of Assisi

7. Juliusspital

The Juliusspital was founded as a hospital and old people's home in 1576 by Prince Bishop Julius Echter von Mespelbrunn. It was the first university clinic and contains Wuerzburg's oldest operating pharmacy, still serving Juliusspital's patients.

In 1895 X-rays were discovered here by Wilhelm Conrad Roentgen.

Like so much else in Wuerzburg, the Juliusspital suffered major damages during the air raid.

8. Kaeppele

The Kaeppele was built by Balthasar Neumann between 1747 and 1750. He built it onto a small chapel that had already existed for about 100 years. It is unusual, with its onion dome shaped cupolas, similar in design to those of the Russian Orthodox churches of the time.

The Kaeppele is a pilgrimage chapel with 365 steps on the foot path leading up to it. Along the way are 14 pavilions with life-size stone statues representing the Stations of the Cross.[35]

The Kaeppele was one of only a few buildings in Wuerzburg to escape the destruction of the World War II air raid.

---

[35] 11-pg 62

9. Lusamgarten

The Lusam Garden was built next to the Neumuenster Church in the 12th century. The pillars and arches in the garden are the originals- they were taken apart, removed, and put in a safe place before the 1945 air raid.

The German minstrel, Walther von der Vogelweide ("Waldorf of the Bird Passage") is buried somewhere in the Lusam Garden. A tombstone there commemorates his burial, but his tomb has never been found. A local legend places the actual tomb closer to the church than where the tombstone is. The story goes that *a little boy climbed the church tower to steal bird's eggs, and fell off. When he fell, he hit his head on Walther's tomb.*

Walther von der Vogelweide is one of the three men on the fountain in front of the Residenz.

10. Marienberg Fortress

Starting with Franconian shell limestone available around the Marienberg, the Prince Bishops of the 12th and 13th centuries began building the strong walls of the fortress that still stand today. One of the next problems to overcome was getting water up to the Marienberg. By the year 1200 the 126 meter well had been drilled, through the rock, down to the river's springs.[36] During Prince Bishop Julius Echter von Mespelbrunn's reign, a Renaissance fountain house was built over the well.[37]

Each succeeding Prince Bishop made the castle their own by redecorating and rebuilding. Prince Bishop von Mespelbrunn made the largest changes in the 16th century. And then in 1650 the Prince's Garden was added, and in 1712 an arsenal was constructed in the shape of an L. The Arsenal included a military hospital and a huge wine cellar, though its primary function was to contain arms and the gun powder.[38]

---

[36] 13-pg 24
[37] 13-pg 4
[38] 13-pg 12

For almost 500 years, from 1253-1720, the Marienberg served as home to Wuerzburg's Prince Bishops.

In 1720, the Prince Bishop moved his home from the castle to across the street from where his new palace, the Residenz, was being built. The castle was then relegated to a merely defensive role.

When Wuerzburg became part of the State of Bavaria in 1803, the holdings of the Prince Bishops (the castle, palace, etc.) were turned over to the state.

Even the great Marienberg Fortress fell victim to the bombs dropped in the air raid of 1945.[39]

---

[39] 13-pg 8

11. Mainfraenkische Museum

In 1947 the Main-Franconian Museum was moved to the Arsenal at the Marienberg. It contains the world's greatest collection of Franconian art, both old and new.

In the Riemenschneider Hall of the Museum one finds a special collection of Tilman Riemenschneider's sculptures. It is in this hall that the full effect of his work can be felt. This collection contains a large number of his statues, and in another part of the Museum is a very large special table Riemenschneider made for the town hall. (Most of the statues by Riemenschneider seen throughout Wuerzburg are actually reproductions, with the originals stored safely in the Museum.)

There are numerous other special treasures waiting to be discovered at the Main-Franconian Museum: The "largest medieval standard (battle flag) in existence in Germany";[40] the first large wooden model of Wuerzburg[41]; to name just a few. The Main-Franconian Museum is the second most toured museum in Bavaria.

---

[40] 8 - pg 8
[41] 11- pg 45

12. Marienkapelle

The Marienkapelle was built as a "citizen's church" ("ein burger kirche"). It was the first church to be built in Wuerzburg that was not directly connected to a Prince Bishop, a monastery, or a convent. It was erected in the 14th and 15th centuries.

The Adam and Eve statues on the side of the church were the first works Riemenschneider sculpted in Wuerzburg. (The originals are in the Museum at the castle). It was unusual for that time to show Adam as a young man.

The front of the church is a relief of "the last judgment", visually depicting the verse that says Christ's "tongue will be like a sword". It shows people coming out of their tombs. On the bottom is the dragon, representing Hell. It shows most of the leaders going to Hell. The left side represents heaven, and shows the people, mainly women, going to Heaven.

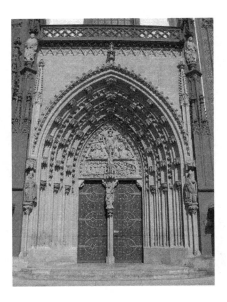

The back side of the church shows the artist's explanation of the Virgin Birth. (Be sure to study it for a few minutes in the picture below!)

Artist's Explanation of the Virgin Birth

The painted altar in the church, on the front side, is the Isenheim Altar.

It is a small copy of the original (which is now in Colmar, France). It was made by Matthias Grunewald, a Wuerzburg-born artist, in about 1518. He is one of the three men shown on the Residenz fountain.

There are countless Madonna statues throughout Wuerzburg, in churches, in private homes, etc. The silver Madonna on the other side of the church was made in Augsburg in 1680, and is very unusual. It was made by the craftsmen of Augsburg, where the silversmiths and goldsmiths of the 16th to 18th centuries were recognized world-wide.[42]

Under the half-burnt statue near the silver Madonna is a stone dedicated to the victims of conquest. It shows these sad dates in Wuerzburg's history:

> 1349-Jewish ghetto destroyed
> 1400-Local war (between Wuerzburg and neighboring area)
> 1525-Peasants' War
> 1631-Thirty Years' War
> 1813-Napolean's battles
> 1945-World War II bombing

The Marienkapelle used to have numerous stained glass windows, and many statues inside, until the bombing.

---

[42] 12-pg 136

13. Balthasar Neumann

Balthasar Neumann came to Wuerzburg in 1711 to become a cannonball maker. He began his career as a military officer before he began his work as an architect. He went on to become "Germany's best known architect of the Baroque".[43] In the next 42 years he designed and oversaw the building of over 100 structures - including palaces, houses, and churches.[44]

One of the magnificent buildings designed by Neumann

From the balcony of his apartment, he could look out over the city he loved, and he could observe the work at the Residenz.

---

[43] 11 - pg 22
[44] 6 - pg 53

14. Neumuenster Church

The Baroque façade of the Neumuenster Church has two entrances: One to the church, and one to the crypt in the basement. It was recently restored. The oval in the center of the façade shows the ascension of the Virgin Mary, with an angel holding her lily. The statue above her represents Christ; and the statue on His right is St. Burkard, first Bishop of Wuerzburg. The statue on His left is Kilian; and to the far right and left are Kolonat and Totnan.

The coat of arms above the door shows the "Franconian rake", the zigzag line representing the city wall, and the combat flag of Wuerzburg, both of which are seen on coat of arms throughout Wuerzburg. The rest of the coat of arms is particular to the family it belonged to.

The crypt (tomb) in the basement contains the relics of Kilian, Kolonat, and Totnan. There is also a well there. Wells were dug in the basements of churches because the church was a place of refuge in times of siege. Invaders usually poisoned the town's water supply, and the well provided the people with a safe source of water.

The crucifix on the left side of the pews was made in the late 14th century. It is an unusual crucifix with Christ's arms folded, like a mother holding a baby. *One story explains that a Swedish solider (during the Thirty Years' War) recognized its worth, and tried to steal it. Christ wrapped His arms around the soldier to prevent him from sinning.*[45]
A second story explains that the artist was trying to express Christ taking the whole world in His arms.

The Madonna on the right side was made by Riemenschneider. Represented as "the queen of heaven", she wears a crown. This statue is made of sandstone.

The statues of Kolonat, Totnan, and Kilian at the front of the Neumuenster Church were originally made by Riemenschneider. A Wuerzburg artist made reproductions of them at the turn of the century. The original statues were burnt during the war and these copies were brought in after the war to replace them. The ceiling frescoes in the Neumuenster also had to be redone by a local artist after the war.

---

[45] 11 - pg 55

15. Old University

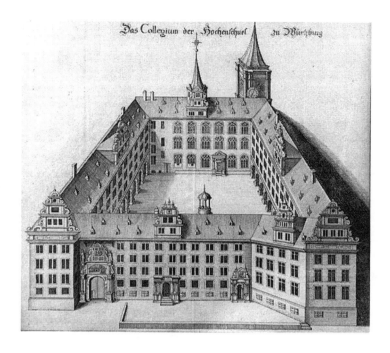

The University was founded in 1403 and then closed by student riots in 1415. It was reopened in 1582 by Prince Bishop Julius Echter von Mespelbrunn. It started with a theological department, and added law and medicine.

Wuerzburg is a university town, but it has no campus. Education departments are located throughout the city. Students must either walk or use bus transportation to get from class to class. 20,000 students attend the graduate school here.

The University Church is an impressive Renaissance church, begun in 1586. Its tower is the highest church tower in Wuerzburg. It is still being rebuilt after its destruction in the war, and is only used now for concerts and lectures. The University Library was totally burnt out during the bombing. After the war, many libraries around the world sent books to get the library going again.

16. Rathaus

The Rathaus was originally the seat of government of the ruling Prince Bishops of Wuerzburg. It became the town hall in 1316, when it was bought from Graff (Count) Eckhart. It is built in both the Romanesque and Renaissance style.

On the front of the Rathaus is painted a beautiful tree. *While one source[46] says merely that the oak tree is "the traditional symbol for a place of government and justice", I prefer the more romantic story I heard.[47] A beautiful tree had grown across from the Rathaus for many years. When it got sick and had to be removed, the mural was painted on the wall of the building so that the people of Wuerzburg would be able to see it forever.*

---

[46] 8
[47] 1

17. Residenz

The Residenz is one of the finest Baroque structures in Europe! It was built for the Prince Bishops of Wuerzburg in the 18th century, follows the plans of Balthasar Neumann.

During the thirty years it took to build the Residenz, there were six different Prince Bishops in Wuerzburg. Two of them preferred the fortified castle on the hill to the idea of a palace, and didn't continue work on it.

Even those who did support the idea of living in a "palace" instead of in a "castle" understood the necessity of fortifications. As part of the plans for the Residenz a tunnel was built up to the Marienberg.[48]

The Residenz only belonged to Wuerzburg's Prince Bishops until the French Revolution in the early 1800's. When Napoleon came to power in Europe, the church lost power and the Prince Bishop was no longer a prince. King Ludwig became the owner of the Residenz, and even lived there for a while.

For more information on the Residenz, see chapter 3.

---

[48] 13 - pg 6

18. Tilman Riemenschneider

Tilman Riemenschneider became known as the "Master of Wuerzburg". He was one of the leading Gothic sculptors, and gave his work a delicacy and beauty that was quite rare for that time. Riemenschneider's sculptures always had very expressive hands with long slender fingers, and a characteristic S line running through the body of the statue (connecting head, shoulder, waist, knee, and foot).

Once Riemenschneider got his workshop started in Wuerzburg, he practically had a factory, with 70 people working for him.

Some of his works in Wuerzburg can be seen at: Neumuenster Church; the Marienkapelle; the Dom; the St. Burkard Church; and the Main-Franconian Museum. And although the largest collection of Riemenschneider's work is here in Wuerzburg, there are many places in other towns as well. Rimpar, Maidbronn, and Volkach are just a few of the nearby places his sculptures and altars can be seen.[49]

A Riemenschneider Altar

---

[49] 9 - pg 4

Riemenschneider's works in the Dom include two tombstones that are part of a series of tombstones made for Wuerzburg's Prince Bishops over a seven century period. The tombstones were not damaged in the air raid because they had previously been covered with plaster of Paris.

In 1521 Riemenschneider was made mayor of Wuerzburg by its citizens. During the Peasants' War he was imprisoned in the castle for some time. Until the 1960s it was believed that his fingers had been broken during this imprisonment, since no artwork had apparently been made by him after that time. Actually, the people were too impoverished to order work from him at that time. In the 1960s it was discovered that he did reconstruction work on an altar in a Kitzingen church during his last years.

A cemetery once existed between the Dom and the Neumuenster Church (in the area that is now the Kilianiplatz). Riemenschneider's tombstone was found in that area in 1822. It had been made by his son. The original is now in the Museum at the Marienberg and a reproduction hangs on the side of the Dom. The words in the middle of it explain that Riemenschneider's son-in-law was buried in the same tomb with him. Both their coats of arms are pictured on the tombstone.

Riemenschneider is the third Wuerzburg artist represented on the Residenz fountain.

Riemenschneider on the Fountain

19. St. Burkard Church

This very large church was consecrated in 1042. It developed from the Monastery founded by Bishop Burkard in 748. The west part is Romanesque and the east building is Late Gothic.

"In 1464 the St. Burkard Monastery became a foundation of an order of Knights."[50]

St. Burkard contains a Riemenschneider Madonna.

This is a Riemenschneider Madonna, though not the one at St. Burkard's.

---

[50] 11 - pg 52

20. World War II

Six weeks before the end of the war, Wuerzburg was bombed. Eighty-five percent of the city was destroyed in the air raid. Most building walls were left standing, but most roofs were destroyed. The insides of buildings were mostly wood and were burned by the bombs. Many of the statutes on the building were saved, because they had been covered with plaster before the air raid.

There have been three reasons suggested for the bombing of Wuerzburg:

1. **Retaliation:** Germany had bombed Coventry, England--a similar city of historical import, with little military significance.

2. **Location:** Many German troops went through Wuerzburg on their way to other places.

3. **Refute Propaganda:** The Allies needed to prove to the Germans that the war was hopeless. With his propaganda, most Germans still thought Hitler could win the war. (Before the end of 1944, only strategic locations had been bombed. At that point the "total war" started, and places like Dresden and Wuerzburg were bombed.)

On the 5th of April, 1945, Americans entered Wuerzburg, (XXI Corps, 7th Army). They called Wuerzburg "the tomb at the Main River". Buildings were still smoking; some were still burning. The damage to the city was so severe it was almost relocated down river at Veitshoechheim.

An American Art Protection Officer (Lt. John Skilton) was appointed to go through Wuerzburg and see what "historic treasures"[51] could be salvaged. Skilton, his soldiers, and some men from Wuerzburg, took tar paper and wood and built a temporary roof over the middle section of the Residenz. Only because of their quick thinking and hard work were Tiepolo's frescoes and Bossi's stucco work preserved. In 1976 Skilton came back to Wuerzburg for a big parade and celebration, and was awarded the highest honor a non-German can receive. "He is honored today as the 'Savior of the Residenz' and his portrait hangs in a passage of the restored palace."[52] In that same hallway is a "sobering exhibit on the bombing and on the restoration work."[53]

12 million refugees fled through Wuerzburg from the east from January to May, 1945. There were lots of jobs for them after the war rebuilding the city.

---

[51] 8 - pg 7
[52] 8 - pg 7
[53] 8 - pg 8

Chapter Three
A Special Look at Wuerzburg's Residenz

Introduction

In the 18th century the Prince Bishop of Wuerzburg saw drawings of Versailles Palace in France.

The Palace of Versailles

He decided he should have a similar, smaller version to live in, instead of the fortress on the hill. Thus began the plans for the Wuerzburg Residenz.

The Prince Bishop had the large sum of money needed to undertake such a grand building plan for two reasons:
1. The Prince Bishop had won the equivalent of 50 million marks in an embezzlement trial
2. A Wuerzburg nobleman had been the pay officer for the Hungarian Mercenary Army. One pay day he went AWOL with the army's money (wagons full of gold and silver) and brought it to Wuerzburg to the Prince Bishop. It took the Prince Bishop's servants all night to get the money from the Pay Officer up the hill to the castle.

The Residenz is one of the biggest and most elaborate Baroque palaces in Germany! It was begun in 1719 by Prince Bishop Johann Philip Franz von Schoenborn. In 1746, the left wing was finally finished, and Prince Bishop Friedrich Karl von Schoenborn moved in. The right wing was finished next, followed by the center section. By then styles had changed, explaining the differences between the sides and the center, including the trim at the top.

The side palaces were for the court and the diplomats. The small floor-between the main floors--was for the builders. The servants were put on the small attic floor. When completed, the Residenz contained 312 rooms and four big halls. The two-floor winery in the basement was once the biggest in Germany.

Six weeks before the air raid of 1945, everything that could be removed from the Residenz was, including tapestries, wall panels, furniture, etc. During the air raid, the side wings of the Residenz burned completely and collapsed; in the middle only the roof burned. It was only because of Balthasar Neumann's arch construction over Tiepolo's great ceiling fresco that the middle section did not also collapse.

Unfortunately, not much of the original furniture is left in the Residenz. The furniture had been moved out to another palace. After World War II, more than 10 million refugees came into Germany escaping from the east. Many moved into the palace which housed the furniture. It was a COLD winter, and the refugees burned more than 2 million marks worth of furniture (most of it from the Wuerzburg Residenz!) for HEAT.

And now for a look at the Residenz:

Northern Apartments   **Garden Hall**   **Southern Apartments**
Imperial Hall (2nd floor)

Carriage Room
White Hall (2nd floor)

Court Chapel

Great Staircase
Ceiling Fresco (above)

1. Garden Hall

This hall was used for garden parties. The current windows weren't originally there and it was very open.

The ceiling fresco here, "The Feast of the Gods", was done by a Wuerzburg artist, Johann Zick, in 1750. It features many mythological gods, including:

a) Argus (3 eyed god)--"Looking at you with Argus eyes", is an expression meaning to stare intently at someone.

b) Cronus (god of death)--He had to be turned around, so he wouldn't be peering down on the guests, but his wings and sickle had already been painted.

c) Diane (the goddess of hunt and moon)--She is shown resting after a knee injury. The artist didn't have much imagination, and many of the characters looked similar. The Prince Bishop was dissatisfied with Zick's work and hired Giovanni Tiepolo from Vienna as his court painter instead.

Wet frescoes were made by putting Plaster of Paris on the ceiling, and painting while it was still wet. This made it difficult to make changes, and is also why colors are so vivid after more than two centuries! The three-dimensional robes and the stucco work that joined into the paintings were the link between art and architecture -- filling the need for **harmony** that was present in the Baroque style. The robes were made by soaking burlap in plaster. When it hardened it was painted. This effect is seen throughout the Residenz.

All of the marble except the free-standing pillars, are stucco work imitation marble, which was more expensive than real marble. The pillars helped hold up the vaulted ceiling in this room, and helped give it a lighter feeling than the Carriage Room next door.

2. Carriage Room

The Carriage Room or Vestibule is where the important party guests were dropped off. This area was made without the supporting columns, so that carriages could get in and out easily.[54] It was also a very open area when the Residenz was built, since the current doors were not there originally. It is decorated with the gods of the underworld. It looks like the gods are "holding up the Residenz". One gets the feeling of going up when heading up the stairs towards the ceiling.

---

[54] 10 - pg 33

3. Great Staircase

Balthasar Neumann became very famous for his work on the Residenz, especially the staircase! When he was done designing it, it was impressive even by French standards, the highest artistic/architectural standards of the day.[55] The lanterns along the staircase are works by Johann Wagner, one of many of the famous artists of that time who worked alongside Neumann.

The steps are half the normal height, so it feels like you are floating instead of marching. Guests would sometimes take an hour to walk up the steps during a party. The Prince Bishop could stand on the balcony and watch his guests; it would look like they were going up on their knees.

---

[55] 10 - pg 35

4. Tiepolo's Ceiling Fresco

Tiepolo called his ceiling fresco over Neumann's great staircase the "Theater of the World". This painting is the largest ceiling fresco in the world done in a single unit. (Michelangelo's fresco at the Sistine Chapel was done in several smaller sections.) It covers more than 6,000 square feet, and shows the whole world honoring the Prince Bishop of Wuerzburg. It took Tiepolo less than 1 year to paint. While he painted, his helpers mixed the colors for him. (When reconstruction work was done to the Residenz, chicken bones were found on the ledges next to the ceiling. Apparently, Tiepolo would spend the entire day working, and his food would be brought up to him!)

The ceiling fresco shows each of the four continents known at that time. Each continent is represented by a girl. The girls in Europe, Africa, and Asia are each pointing at the Prince Bishop. The girl in America points at the Prince Bishop's flag. The figures in the fresco have duo meanings - 1) religion and 2) history/mythology.

a. Africa (right)-continent of merchandise

- Africa is represented by a Jewelry seller.

b. America (front)--continent of nature and hunting

- America is shown with Indian hats (from India) and cannibals. (Showing the misconceptions about America in 18th century Europe!)

c. Asia (left)-continent of religion

- Asia has crosses, a pyramid, and a stone with Armenian script. –The girl standing under the pyramid represents the Virgin

Mary and Cleopatra. (It shows the goddess of fertility defeated, lying at her feet.) --The pyramid seems to shift as the viewer moves.

d. Europe (back)-continent of art

- The paintress is pointing to Wuerzburg, "the center of the world"
- Musicians
- Man in Ivory Coat
  i. Poet
  ii. Oegg--Italian artist who made the wrought-iron gates
      (He was a blacksmith known for making tomb crosses in Italy)
- Man on cannon--the Art of War
  i. The artillery colonel (Col. Neumann, the self-made architect)
  ii. There was skepticism that the ceiling could exist without support, so a cannon was shot to see if the ceiling would fall down (since it was only 20 centimeters thick). They say Neumann had his family and their belongings on a hill overlooking the city when the cannon was shot (just in case the ceiling didn't hold).

74

Tiepolo is the artist depicted in the corner wearing a (yellow) scarf:

e. Center section

- The figure in the middle represents Christ welcoming the Prince Bishop to heaven.
- Mercury
- Rainbow contains the Zodiac signs

5. White Hall

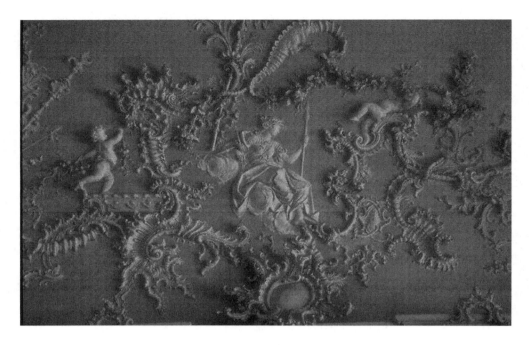

Stucco Work in the White Hall

The White Hall was a ballroom which offered a contrast between the brilliant colors of Tiepolo's "Theater of the World" and the colors to follow in the Imperial Room.

The walls of the White Hall were done by Antonio Bossi with stucco war scenes. And the stucco work was continued up the walls to the ceiling. This is the style of stucco work that became famous as "Wuerzburger Rocco".[56] Bossi, an Italian artist, did the work in this room in less than nine months. He couldn't leave the room until he was finished. There was a hurry to get it done before Maria Theresa, the Austrian empress, visited in 1745. Since he was in such a hurry, Bossi worked freehand, without even sketches to work from! It is

---

[56] 2 - pg 56

said that he went blind as a result of his work at the Residenz,[57] and "died insane in 1766".[58]

It took modern day artisans four years to redo one corner of the stucco work marred by water damage when a fire on the roof was extinguished. From this ballroom the Prince Bishop could see the Schoenborn Tomb Chapel, where he knew he would someday end up! On the walls hang portraits of the Residenz.

In the chandeliers, the purple glass is old, while the yellow glass is new. The White Hall had real candles until recently. The shadows from the candles made beautiful shadows on the stucco work.

---

[57] 1
[58] 10 - pg 39

6. Imperial Hall ("Kaisersaal")

The Imperial Hall is one of the crowning achievements of the Residenz--bringing together Bossi's stucco work, Tiepolo's ceiling frescoes, and Neumann's architecture. "What these artists created is a joint work of art."[59] The ceiling arches Neumann created in this room added a special effect to this already regal setting.

The oval fresco in the center shows Emperor Barbarossa. The young lady being carried in Apollo's sun wagon is Beatrice of Burgundy coming to Wuerzburg for her marriage to Barbarossa. The wedding occurred in the 12th century, but the figures are dressed in 18th century style. And the Prince Bishop shown is one from the 18th century.

One of the side frescoes shows a representative of the state kneeling to a representative of the church for the wedding. As balance it was necessary to have the opposite side portray the representative of the church kneeling to the representative of the state in a ceremony where a Prince Bishop was being installed.

These frescoes at the Residenz gave Tiepolo much-deserved fame.

---

[59] 10 - pg 43

7. The Southern Imperial Apartments (right side wing)

The rooms in both side wings were destroyed in the air raid. The wings have been recently reopened after considerable time and money was spent to reconstruct them. Fortunately, many detailed photographs existed, enabling the restorers to bring back most of the original effects.

a. Antechamber (1st Alexander Hall)
- The tapestries were woven in 1700 and brought down from the Marienberg. They had to be altered the walls here.
- The chandeliers here: one is original, one is a replacement. (The new one cost 24 times what the original had cost.)
- The paintings on the ceiling were borrowed from a Munich museum.
- The stucco ceiling took 100,000 marks to replace (about $400,000 at the time).

b. Audience Chamber
- The tapestries show scenes from Alexander the Great's battles.
- These are the original panels and mirrors.
- Skilton found the stoves in pieces, and had the pieces saved so they could be reconstructed.

c. Venetian Room (Emperor's Bedroom)
- The tapestries show scenes from the carnival in Venice.
- The little panels along the bottom of the walls were done by local court painters.
- The sleeping knights and noblemen on the ceiling are new. There were complaints about the colors in the 1960s when this wing was opened.
- The game table was done with reverse-glass painting (a very difficult process).

79

d. Mirror Hall

Mirrors in the form of mirrored cabinets and mirrored walls were popular during the Baroque and Rococo building eras. Because of this, Mirror Hall was an important part of the Residenz. Neumann and Bossi again combined their creative efforts, and with the aid of several other craftsmen created the Mirror Hall over a five year period (1740 to 1745). They had <u>just</u> completed it when Empress Maria Theresa visited.

200 years after it was completed, the Mirror Hall was destroyed. For many years the task of restoring this wonderful room was thought to be impossible. Finally, in 1979, a Wuerzburg artist, Wolfgang Lentz, and his helpers were able to begin the task. (They had done much of the reconstruction work on other parts of the Residenz by this time.) For the next eight years they worked--using pictures and a single piece of the original. (It had broken off when someone had tried to remove the mirrors before the air raid.) The reconstruction of this one room cost eight million marks.

The Hall shows the four continents in the ceiling corners.

8. The Northern Imperial Apartments

This was almost totally reconstructed in 1990; at a cost of more than 30 million marks (over $100,000).

a. Antechamber (2nd Alexander Hall)

- It also shows scenes from the battles of Alexander the Great.

b. Audience Chamber (3rd Alexander Hall)

- The B&B tapestries are from Belgium.
- The desk was made of rosewood and ivory. It took a craftsman more than eight years to make it, and then he gave it to the Prince Bishop as a gift.
- The white panels are not original.

c. Red Cabinet Room

- The silk tapestries on the wall are French. Restorers went back to France and the company which made them originally still had the original patterns.

d. Green Cabinet Room

- The two tapestries on opposite walls show the four continents.
- The portraits are of the grandparents of Marie Antoinette, the parents of Maria Theresa. They changed the constitution so Maria Theresa could become ruler of Austria, since they had no son.

e. Napoleon's Bedroom

- Napoleon stayed in Wuerzburg on some of his travels. He said the Residenz was "the prettiest house of a priest in the world".

- The stucco roses look like porcelain.
- The sun dial depicts Cronus, the god of time and death.

f. 1st Guest Room

- The stove was reconstructed around its original parts.
- Each square meter of the tapestries took one person one year to make.
    - o 1. (left)-shows earth and fire
    - o 2. (right)-shows air and water
- The dresser was inlaid with different colors of wood; only the green was painted.

g. 2nd Guest Room (Tea Room)

- Much white and gold were used in this room to give it a light feeling, leading to the next room.

h. Green Lacquered Room

- The Green Room is the link between the park and the building.
- It was painted like carriages were painted--on silver leaf.
- It was originally done from 1769 to 1744; and was redone from 1969 to 1974.

9. Court Chapel (Hofkirche)

The chapel was built between 1732 and 1738, during the Baroque and Rococo periods. It is decorated with marble, gold, and frescoes. The important Baroque element of symmetry is hard to discern in the building of the chapel, mirrors were placed on the inside wall, to reflect the light coming in from the windows.

The top altar (Mary's altar) was the family altar and the lower altar (Christ's altar) was for services. The fresco above Mary's altar shows the three missionaries being killed. The side altars have paintings above them that Tiepolo did in the winter time (since he couldn't work on ceiling frescoes during the cold weather). The paintings above the right altar shows the ascension of Mary and the painting above the left altar shows the condemnation of an angel. The statue on the left side of the left altar is the Virgin Mary, with a lily. The turned pillars were made to resemble pillars in Solomon's temple.

After the air raid in World War II, the Residenz Chapel suffered much damage from fire and water. Two million marks (almost $8 million) worth of reconstruction was done on the chapel alone. When the fire on the chapel roof was extinguished, all the little gold decorations fell off. They were replaced in 1947 with American tooth plaster.

10. Court Garden (Hofgarten)

Although the gardens were included in the original plans for the Residenz, they were a lower priority than the actual building. As such, work on them was not even begun until almost 30 years later, when the building was near completion. The Residenz gardens were made to look like they continued beyond the city wall.

Since the gardens were limited in size by the city fortifications behind the Residenz, the usual French design was not possible. The smaller section behind the Residenz was to be done in the Italian style, and the larger sections to the side of the Residenz were to be done in the Austrian style of the day. But by time the gardens were done, English landscaping had changed the world of garden planning, and the gardens followed the English style more than any other.[60]

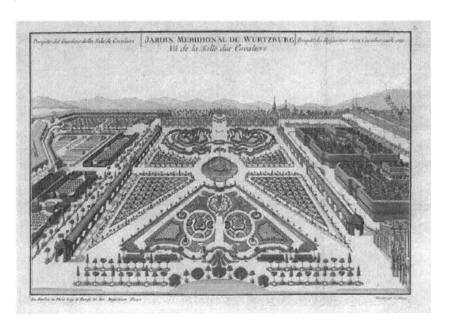

The Gardens in 1770

---

[60] 10 - pgs 21 - 28

The Prince Bishops' summer palace in Veitshoechheim was expanded during the same time period the Garden at the Residenz was completed. The vast gardens in Veitshoechheim made up for the limited ones at the Residenz!

Summer Palace with Gardens at Veitshoechheim

11. Residenz Conclusion

The Wuerzburg Residenz is certainly one of Germany's special treasures. In 1982, it was listed in UNESCO's "List of the World's Inheritance", and brought under its protection.[61] UNESCO is an agency of the United Nations-the United Nations Educational, Scientific and Cultural Organization. It "tries to acquaint the public with important works of art and literature".[62] Only three buildings in Germany are on UNESCO's list-the Residenz in Wuerzburg and two cathedrals.

---

[61] 2 - pg 36
[62] 3-UV- pg 16

Conclusion to the Second Edition

I hope you have enjoyed this brief look at an amazing city, filled with glimpses of history and fantastic art and architecture. Wuerzburg is one of many cities worldwide that enable us to appreciate man's history in an urban setting that showcases human personality and God-given talents.

Of course, it is not meant to be the last word on Wuerzburg, but I hope it was a pleasant <u>introduction</u> to the history of this amazing city, and Germany's history as a whole.

This book was originally written for those who lived in the area of Wuerzburg. With the power of the internet today, including great sources of free pictures like Wikipedia and Creative Commons, this version has been illustrated, to make it easier for those who do not have the privilege of visiting this beautiful German city to enjoy its story, and appreciate its fascinating history...European cities have taken centuries to evolve into their current state, and their histories are far more complicated than their American counterparts. This is part of Wuerzburg's fascination for me.

Appendix 1: References

1. Helga Hoeffner's tours of Wuerzburg (between 1986-1989)

2. Wuerzburg-a living city by W. Sauer, U. Strauch
© 1988 (English and French version) currently available downtown for 12 DMS-good information and great pictures

3. World Book Encyclopedia-1967 edition
articles such as "Peasants' War", "Bubonic Plaque", "Architectural Styles", "Reformation", etc.

4. Germany-A Phaidon Cultural Guide © 1986

5. Michelin Tourist Guide to Germany (6th edition)

6. Castles of Germany-A Stars & Stripes Publication © 1980

7. Cities of Germany-A Stars & Stripes Publication (revised 1977)

8. Pillars & Posts Welcome edition 1989-1990

9. Riemenschneider in Franken text von Hanswernfried Muth (text in English, French, and German)

10. Residenz-Wuerzburg (English Edition)

11. Wuerzburg-Official Guide to the Sights
written by Max H. von Freeding, translated by Irene Ratsch

12. Augsburg: 2,000 years-The Jubilee Book
Edited by Willy Schweinberger ©1985

13. The Fortress Marienberg-Wuerzburg
by Dr Rudolf Edwin Kuhn © 1978

14. Highlights of German History
Text: Dr. Hans Bernhard Graf von Schwienitz
Special USAREUR Library Program Edition

Appendix 2: Timeline

General Germany:		Specific to Wuerzburg:	
~500 -1500	Middle Ages	689	St. Killian Martyred
		706	Marienkirche Built on Hilltop
		742	Bishop Burkard, 1st Bishop in Wuerzburg
768-814	Charlemagne ruled German Empire	788	1st Cathedral Dedicated (by Charlemagne)
800	Charlemagne made Emperor of Germany		
843	Treaty of Verdun (Separated Germany and France)		
1000	End of "Dark Ages"	1000	First City Wall built around Wuerzburg
		1030	Wuerzburg given rights as city in German Empire
		1042	St. Burkard Church consecrated
1050-1250	Romanesque style	1050	Construction begun on the Dom church
1096-99	First Crusade	1133	First stone bridge built over the Main
1147-49	Second Crusade		
1152-90	Barbarossa ruled German Empire	1156	Emperor Barbarossa married in Wuerzburg
		1168	Barbarossa began Prince Bishops in Wuerzburg
		1188	Dom finally consecrated
1189-92	Third Crusade		
1198-1214	Civil War in Germany over Next Ruler	1200	Grafeneckart Built
1201-04	Fourth Crusade	1201	Foundation of Marienberg begun
		1221	Franciscan Monastery founded
1250-73	The great "Interregnum"	1253	Bishops began residing in Marienberg
1250-1500	Gothic style	1316	Rathaus established in the Grafeneckart
1300-50	Gunpowder developed	1319	Buergerspital founded

1334-51	Bubonic Plague in Europe	**1348**	Black Plague in Wuerzburg
		1377	Marienkapelle begun by Townspeople
		1397	King Wenceslas (of Poland) visited Wuerzburg
1447	Gutenberg printed the first book	**1473**	Alte Mainbrucke rebuilt
		1483	Riemenschneider came to Wuerzburg
1500-1600	German Renaissance /End of Middle Ages		
1517	The Reformation began	**1518**	Martin Luther visited Wuerzburg
		1521	Riemenschneider elected Mayor
1524-26	Peasants' War	**1576**	Prince Bishop Mespelbrunn founded Juliusspital
		1582	Old University founded by Mespelbrunn
1600-1800	Baroque style	**1600**	Many additions to Marienberg by Mespelbrunn
1618-48	Thirty Years' War	**1631**	Marienberg stormed by Swedes during war
		1642	First Schoenborn elected Prince Bishop (began big building spree in Wuerzburg)
		1719	Neumann began work on the Residenz
		1724	1st Statues added to the Alte Mainbrucke
		1748	Kaeppele built by Neumann
		1751	Tiepolo painted Residenz frescoes
		1773	Alter Kranen built by Neumann's son
1799-1813	Napoleonic Wars	**1806**	Napoleon stayed at the Residenz
		1815-1825	Crown Prince King Ludwig in Wuerzburg
1870-71	Bismarck united Germany	**1871**	City Wall torn down, moat filled in
		1895	X-rays discovered at Juliusspital
1914-18	World War I		
1939-45	World War II	**Mar 1945**	Wuerzburg bombed

Appendix 3: Map of Wuerzburg

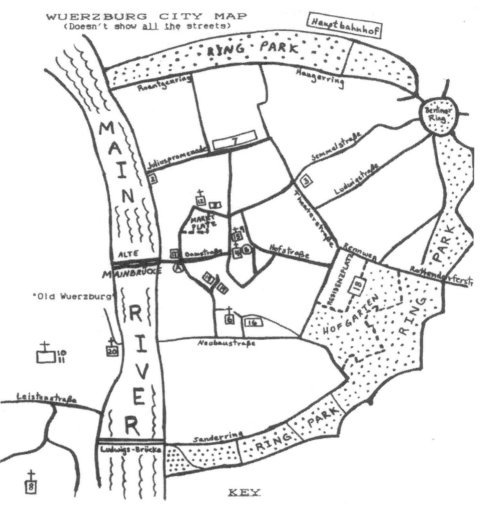

WUERZBURG CITY MAP
(Doesn't show all the streets)

KEY

2. Alter Kranen
3. Buergerspital
4. Dom
5. Falkenhaus
6. Franciscan Monastery
7. Juliusspital
8. Kappele
9. Lusamgarten
10. Mainfraenkische Museum
11. Marienberg Fortress

12. Marienkappelle
14. Neumuen's House
15. Neumuenster Church
16. Old University
17. Rathaus
18. Residenz
19. Riemenschneider's House
20. St. Burkard Church
 A. Four Pipes Fountain
 B. Kilianiplatz